core belief
Bible Study Series
for senior high

WHY Relationships MATTER

Loveland, Colorado

Why Relationships Matter
Core Belief Bible Study Series
Copyright © 1998 Group Publishing, Inc.

All rights reserved. No part of this book may be reproduced in any manner whatsoever without prior written permission from the publisher, except where noted in the text and in the case of brief quotations embodied in critical articles and reviews. For information, write Permissions, Group Publishing, Inc., Dept. PD, P.O. Box 481, Loveland, CO 80539.

Credits
Editor: Karl Leuthauser
Creative Development Editors: Ivy Beckwith and Paul Woods
Chief Creative Officer: Joani Schultz
Copy Editor: Candace McMahan
Art Director: Ray Tollison
Cover Art Director: Jeff A. Storm
Computer Graphic Artist/Illustrator: Eris Klein
Photographer: Jafe Parsons
Production Manager: Gingar Kunkel

Unless otherwise noted, Scripture taken from the HOLY BIBLE, NEW INTERNATIONAL VERSION®. Copyright © 1973, 1978, 1984 by International Bible Society. Used by permission of Zondervan Publishing House. All rights reserved.

ISBN 0-7644-0896-8

10 9 8 7 6 5 4 3   07 06 05 04 03 02 01

Printed in the United States of America.

Visit our Web site: www.grouppublishing.com

Bible Study Series
for senior high

contents:

the Core Belief: Relationships

God created us to live in relationship with one another, and he created a variety of relationships for us to enjoy—family, friends, co-workers, and neighbors. Being in relationship with others carries obligations, and we should all grant one another basic considerations such as love, respect, honesty, and forgiveness. As Christians, our goal is to love, serve, and support one another and to strive to maintain positive relationships with non-Christians to draw them into relationship with Jesus Christ.

the Helpful Stuff

RELATIONSHIPS AS A CORE CHRISTIAN BELIEF **7**
(or Why the Lone Ranger Is Seen Only on Cable)

ABOUT CORE BELIEF BIBLE STUDY SERIES **10**
(or How to Move Mountains in One Hour or Less)

WHY ACTIVE AND INTERACTIVE LEARNING WORKS WITH TEENAGERS **55**
(or How to Keep Your Kids Awake)

YOUR EVALUATION **61**
(or How You Can Edit Our Stuff Without Getting Paid)

the Studies

A Friend Indeed — 15
THE ISSUE: Friendship
THE BIBLE CONNECTION: Proverbs 13:20; 15:1; 16:18; 17:17; Romans 15:2; 16:17-18; and 1 Corinthians 15:33-34
THE POINT: Choose your friends wisely.

Trust Me — 25
THE ISSUE: Trust
THE BIBLE CONNECTION: Genesis 22:1-19; 27:1-29
THE POINT: Trust is earned.

Teenage Romance — 35
THE ISSUE: Dating
THE BIBLE CONNECTION: Matthew 1:18-25; and Luke 1:26-38; 2:1-21
THE POINT: Relationships take work and commitment.

Sex Worth Waiting For — 45
THE ISSUE: Sexual Abstinence
THE BIBLE CONNECTION: Proverbs 5:3-8, 15-17; Song of Songs 4:1-7; 5:10-16; 8:6-7; 1 Corinthians 6:18-20; and 1 Thessalonians 4:3-8
THE POINT: Sex creates a bond that thrives only in marriage.

Relationships as a Core Christian Belief

Nothing in the world brings a smile to young people as quickly as seeing the face of someone they love. Unfortunately, nothing hurts quite as deeply as losing that love when people leave or relationships fail. So kids are faced with a constant struggle. Since relationships can be a powerful source of pleasure and happiness, all young people want and need them. However, because those same relationships can fail and produce broken hearts and bitter tears, kids sometimes avoid them or enter into them only halfheartedly. Nevertheless, one fact remains: Your kids need relationships. They need intimacy, vulnerability, trust, acceptance, challenge—all the qualities that only close relationships can bring.

Your teenagers are looking for positive relationships. One of the first places they look is in their **friendships**. The first study in the book will help kids to understand the importance of friendship and to see that friends have a strong influence on their lives. It will remind kids of how important it is to choose their friends wisely.

The second study in this book will help kids learn what it takes to become a good friend. Healthy relationships are based on **trust**. This study will help kids see that since trust is earned, they must work on their relationships by building trust with others.

The third study addresses a topic that is on just about every teenager's mind. The lesson will lead kids in an honest discussion on **dating**. Students will be challenged to think about what dating is all about and will discover that relationships take work and commitment.

The final study in this book addresses **sexual abstinence**. Kids receive so many confusing messages about sex, and they need to understand God's design for sex. Students will learn how sex affects relationships and why God designed sex for marriage.

Young people need someone to show them how to develop healthy and lasting relationships. Using the studies within this Core Christian Belief, you'll be able to teach and model biblical principles for forming good relationships with others.

For a more comprehensive look at this Core Christian Belief, read Group's **Get Real: Making Core Christian Beliefs Relevant to Teenagers.**

DEPTHFINDER: WHAT THE BIBLE TEACHES ABOUT RELATIONSHIPS

To help you effectively guide your kids toward this Core Christian Belief, use these overviews as a launching point for a more in-depth study of relationships.

- **God wants us to live in relationship with others.** God didn't create us to live alone. We're social beings. Our most important relationship is with God, but we also need significant relationships with other people to enjoy life as God intended (Genesis 2:18; Deuteronomy 6:4-5; Ecclesiastes 4:9-12; Song of Songs 8:6-7; and 1 Corinthians 12:20-21).
- **God established a variety of human relationships.** Since people are different, their relationship needs will be different. Even a person's individual needs will be different during the various stages of his or her life. Still, people generally need a variety of relationships with family, friends, co-workers, and neighbors (Leviticus 19:18, 33-34; Proverbs 17:17; 18:22, 24; 1 Corinthians 7:1-7; and 2 Thessalonians 3:6-13).
- **Every relationship carries obligations.** Certain responsibilities go along with particular relationships. For example, parents should nurture their children, husbands and wives should remain faithful to each other, and employees and employers should treat each other fairly (Exodus 20:2-17; Matthew 7:9-11; Ephesians 5:21–6:9; and Philippians 2:3-4).
- **Because all people are equal before God, they should grant each other certain basic considerations.** The Bible instructs us to *love* everyone—including our enemies—as we love ourselves. We're to treat all people with respect and allow those around us a reasonable amount of *freedom* to make their own choices. In addition, we're to be *honest* at all times and be willing to extend *forgiveness* to others because God has forgiven us (Genesis 1:26-27; Proverbs 12:17-22; 14:21; Matthew 6:14-15; Romans 14:1-12; Ephesians 4:25; and 1 Peter 2:17).
- **Christians should love, serve, and support one another.** God has created the body of Christ to be a community of Christians who share their lives with one another.

Consequently, we should come together regularly to worship God and minister to each other in humility, kindness, compassion, and encouragement (Acts 2:43-45; Romans 12:3-8; Galatians 5:13-14; Ephesians 4:11-16, 29-32; and Hebrews 10:23-25).

- **Christians should maintain positive relationships with non-Christians.** God doesn't want Christians to remove themselves from the world. Rather, we're to form relationships with non-Christians, show love to them, and tell them about God's love for them in Jesus Christ. Our lives should draw non-Christians to God (Matthew 5:43-47; 28:18-20; Hebrews 12:14; James 1:27; and 1 Peter 2:11-12).
- **Conflict in relationships is inevitable.** Since we don't live in an ideal world, we'll experience the effects of damaged and broken relationships. The causes of conflict in relationships vary, including such things as misunderstanding, sin, and differing personalities (Genesis 3:14-19; Acts 15:36-41; 1 Corinthians 1:10-17; and Galatians 2:11-14).
- **It's important to resolve conflict.** When we experience conflict with someone, we should continue to grant that person the basic considerations due all people. We can try to resolve the conflict by discussing the problem one-to-one, offering a reasonable solution, or asking for the help of other Christians. In some instances, however, the only way to avoid ongoing conflict may be to break off a relationship (Genesis 13:1-12; Proverbs 15:1; 17:9; Matthew 5:23-26; 18:15-35; 1 Corinthians 6:1-8; 7:12-16; and Titus 3:9-10).

CORE CHRISTIAN BELIEF OVERVIEW

Here are the twenty-four Core Christian Belief categories that form the backbone of Core Belief Bible Study Series:

The Nature of God	Jesus Christ	The Holy Spirit
Humanity	Evil	Suffering
Creation	The Spiritual Realm	The Bible
Salvation	Spiritual Growth	Personal Character
God's Justice	Sin & Forgiveness	The Last Days
Love	The Church	Worship
Authority	Prayer	Family
Service	Relationships	Sharing Faith

Look for Group's Core Belief Bible Study Series books in these other Core Christian Beliefs!

about Core Belief Bible Study Series for senior high

Think for a moment about your young people. When your students walk out of your youth program after they graduate from junior high or high school, what do you want them to know? What foundation do you want them to have so they can make wise choices?

You probably want them to know the essentials of the Christian faith. You want them to base everything they do on the foundational truths of Christianity. Are you meeting this goal?

If you have any doubt that your kids will walk into adulthood knowing and living by the tenets of the Christian faith, then you've picked up the right book. All the books in Group's Core Belief Bible Study Series encourage young people to discover the essentials of Christianity and to put those essentials into practice. Let us explain…

What Is Group's Core Belief Bible Study Series?

Group's Core Belief Bible Study Series is a biblically in-depth study series for junior high and senior high teenagers. This Bible study series utilizes four defining commitments to create each study. These "plumb lines" provide structure and continuity for every activity, study, project, and discussion. They are:

● **A Commitment to Biblical Depth**—Core Belief Bible Study Series is founded on the belief that kids not only *can* understand the deeper truths of the Bible but also *want* to understand them. Therefore, the activities and studies in this series strive to explain the "why" behind every truth we explore. That way, kids learn principles, not just rules.

● **A Commitment to Relevance**—Most kids aren't interested in abstract theories or doctrines about the universe. They want to know how to live successfully right now, today, in the heat of problems they can't ignore. Because of this, each study connects a real-life need with biblical principles that speak directly to that need. This study series finally bridges the gap between Bible truths and the real-world issues kids face.

● **A Commitment to Variety**—Today's young people have been raised in a sound bite world. They demand variety. For that reason, no two meetings in this study series are shaped exactly the same.

● **A Commitment to Active and Interactive Learning**—Active learning is learning by doing. Interactive learning simply takes active learning a step further by having kids teach each other what they've learned. It's a process that helps kids internalize and remember their discoveries.

For a more detailed description of these concepts, see the section titled "Why Active and Interactive Learning Works With Teenagers" beginning on page 55.

So how can you accomplish all this in a set of four easy-to-lead Bible studies? By weaving together various "power" elements to produce a fun experience that leaves kids challenged and encouraged.

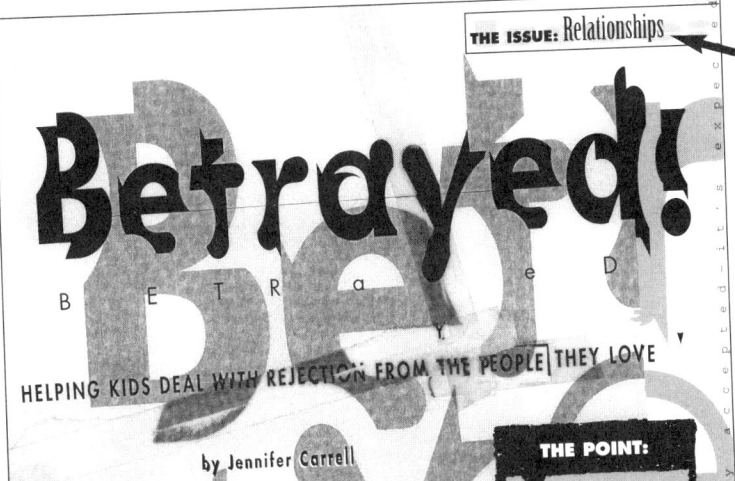

- **A Relevant Topic**—More than ever before, kids live in the now. What matters to them and what attracts their hearts is what's happening in their world at this moment. For this reason, every Core Belief Bible Study focuses on a particular hot topic that kids care about.

- **A Core Christian Belief**—Group's Core Belief Bible Study Series organizes the wealth of Christian truth and experience into twenty-four Core Christian Belief categories. These twenty-four headings act as umbrellas for a collection of detailed beliefs that define Christianity and set it apart from the world and every other religion. Each book in this series features one Core Christian Belief with lessons suited for junior high or senior high students.

  "But," you ask, "won't my kids be bored talking about all these spiritual beliefs?" No way! As a youth leader, you know the value of using hot topics to connect with young people. Ultimately teenagers talk about issues because they're searching for meaning in their lives. They want to find the one equation that will make sense of all the confusing events happening around them. Each Core Belief Bible Study answers that need by connecting a hot topic with a powerful Christian principle. Kids walk away from the study with something more solid than just the shifting ebb and flow of their own opinions. They walk away with a deeper understanding of their Christian faith.

- **The Point**—This simple statement is designed to be the intersection between the Core Christian Belief and the hot topic. Everything in the study ultimately focuses on The Point so that kids study it and allow it time to sink into their hearts.

- **The Study at a Glance**—A quick look at this chart will tell you what kids will do, how long it will take them to do it, and what supplies you'll need to get it done.

Helpful Stuff   11

THE POINT OF *BETRAYED!*:

God is love.

THE BIBLE CONNECTION

1 JOHN 4:7-21 — The Apostle John explains the nature and definition of perfect love.

In this study, kids will compare the imperfect love defined in real-life stories of betrayal to God's definition of perfect love.

By making this comparison, kids can discover that God is love and therefore incapable of betraying them. Then they'll be able to recognize the incredible opportunity God offers to experience the only relationship worthy of their absolute trust.

Explore the verses in The Bible Connect...
mation in the Depthfinder boxes throughout...
understanding of how these Scriptures con...

THE STUDY

DISCUSSION STARTER ▼

Jump-Start (up to 5 minutes) As kids arrive, ask them to th... common themes in movies, books, TV sho... have kids each contribute ideas for a mas... sider providing copies of People magazine to... what's currently showing on television or at... their suggestions, write their responses on ne... come up with a lot of great id... ent, look through this list and try to disc... ments most of these themes have in com...

After kids make several suggestions, menti... responses are connected with the idea of bet...

● Why do you think betrayal is such a...

Betrayed! 17

● **The Bible Connection**—This is the power base of each study. Whether it's just one verse or several chapters, The Bible Connection provides the vital link between kids' minds and their hearts. The content of each Core Belief Bible Study reflects the belief that the true power of God—the power to expose, heal, and change kids' lives—is contained in his Word.

LEADER TIP for The Study

Because this topic can be so powerful and relevant to kids' lives, your group members may be tempted to get caught up in issues and lose sight of the deeper biblical principle found in The Point. Help your kids grasp The Point by guiding kids to focus on the biblical investigation and discussing how God's truth connects with reality in their lives.

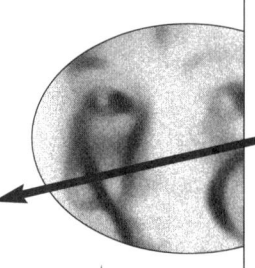

DEPTHFINDER — UNDERSTANDING INTEGRITY

Your students may not be entirely familiar with the meaning of integrity, especially as it might apply to God's character in the Trinity. Use these definitions (taken from Webster's II New Riverside Dictionary) and other information to help you guide kids toward a better understanding of how God maintains integrity through the three expressions of the Trinity.

Integrity: 1. Firm adherence to a code or standard of values. 2. The state of being unimpaired. 3. The quality or condition of being undivided.

Synonyms for integrity include probity, completeness, wholeness, soundness, and perfection.

Our word "integrity" comes from the Latin word *integritas*, which means soundness. *Integritas* is also the root of the word "integer," which means "whole or complete," as in a "whole" number.

The Hebrew word that's often translated "integrity" (for example, in Psalm 25:21 [NIV]) is *tam*. It means whole, perfect, sincere, and honest.

● **Depthfinder Boxes**— These informative sidelights located throughout each study add insight into a particular passage, word, historical fact, or Christian doctrine. Depthfinder boxes also provide insight into teen culture, adolescent development, current events, and philosophy.

CREATIVE GOD-EXPLORATION ▼

Top Hats (18 to 20 minutes) Form three groups, with each trio member from the previous activity going to a different group. Give each group Bibles, paper, and pens, and assign each group a different hat God wears: Father, Son, or Holy Spirit...

● **Leader Tips**— These handy information boxes coach you through the study, offering helpful suggestions on everything from altering activities for different-sized groups to streamlining discussions to using effective discipline techniques.

holy Profiles

Your assigned Bible passage describes how a particular person or group responded when confronted with God's holiness. Use the information in your passage to help your group discuss the questions below. Then use your flashlights to teach the other two groups what you discover.

■ Based on your passage, what does holiness look like?

■ What does holiness sound like?

■ When people see God's holiness, how does it affect them?

■ How is this response to God's holiness like humility?

■ Based on your passage, how would you describe humility?

■ Why is humility an appropriate human response to God's holiness?

■ Based on what you see in your passage, do you think you are a humble person? Why or why not?

■ What's one way you could develop humility in your life this week?

Permission to photocopy this handout from Group's Core Belief Bible Study Series granted for local church use. Copyright © Group Publishing, Inc., Box 481, Loveland, CO 80539.

● **Handouts**—Most Core Belief Bible Studies include photocopiable handouts to use with your group. Handouts might take the form of a fun game, a lively discussion starter, or a challenging study page for kids to take home—anything to make your study more meaningful and effective.

Helpful Stuff 12

The Last Word on Core Belief Bible Studies

Soon after you begin to use Group's Core Belief Bible Study Series, you'll see signs of real growth in your group members. Your kids will gain a deeper understanding of the Bible and of their own Christian faith. They'll see more clearly how a relationship with Jesus affects their daily lives. And they'll grow closer to God.

But that's not all. You'll also see kids grow closer to one another.

That's because this series is founded on the principle that Christian faith grows best in the context of relationship. Each study uses a variety of interactive pairs and small groups and always includes discussion questions that promote deeper relationships. The friendships kids will build through this study series will enable them to grow *together* toward a deeper relationship with God.

THE ISSUE: Friendship

A FRIEND INDEED

by Lara M. Johnson

■ We *all* want to be loved, appreciated, and accepted. But teenagers feel a desperate need to be accepted by everyone. This need beckons teenagers to become whatever their peers expect of them. Jesus has called us to point others to God by what we do and say. Unfortunately, "fitting in" often forces us to compromise this calling. ■ Your students need the support of those around them. They need friends who will help them stand for Jesus in a hostile world. It's easy to find friends who will pull them down and away from Christ. So use this study to encourage your students to choose their friends wisely. Teach them to strive for intimate relationships that challenge them to grow in Christ rather than to fit in with the crowd.

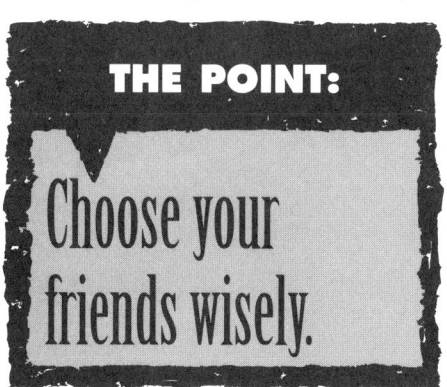

THE POINT: Choose your friends wisely.

The Study
AT A GLANCE

SECTION	MINUTES	WHAT STUDENTS WILL DO	SUPPLIES
Creative Interaction	10 to 15	SOCIALIZE—Interact according to assigned behaviors and discuss how the behaviors can affect friendship.	Bibles, "Behavior" handouts (p. 23), scissors
Bible Exploration	15 to 20	FAMOUS FRIENDS—Make lists of different types of people and discuss what it would be like to be friends with those people.	Bible, newsprint, tape, markers
Personal Evaluation	10 to 15	YOUR FRIENDS—Evaluate their choice of friends.	Bibles, pens, paper
Active Closing	10 to 15	UP AND DOWN—Play a game in which they are pulled up or down.	

notes:

THE POINT OF "A FRIEND INDEED":

Choose your friends wisely.

THE BIBLE CONNECTION

PROVERBS 16:18	This verse addresses some negative aspects of pride.
PROVERBS 13:20; 15:1; 17:17; ROMANS 15:2; 16:17-18; and 1 CORINTHIANS 15:33-34	These passages address important aspects of friendship.

In this study, students will interact according to different assigned behaviors, look at different "types" of friends, evaluate their own choice of friends, and play a game in which they attempt to pull each other to different locations.

Through this experience, teenagers can discover that our friends affect who we are and who we become and that we should choose our friends wisely.

Explore the verses in The Bible Connection; then examine the information in the Depthfinder boxes throughout the study to gain a deeper understanding of how these Scriptures connect with your young people.

THE STUDY

LEADER TIP for The Study

Because this topic can be so powerful and relevant to kids' lives, your group members may be tempted to get caught up in issues and lose sight of the deeper biblical principle found in The Point. Help your kids grasp The Point by guiding kids to focus on the biblical investigation and discussing how God's truth connects with reality in their lives.

CREATIVE INTERACTION ▼

Socialize (10 to 15 minutes) As students arrive, give each one a section of the "Behavior" handout (p. 23).

Say: **Read the Scripture on your handout and the behavior that corresponds to that Scripture. For the next five minutes, I'd like you to act according to the behavior described on your handout. For example, if the behavior described on your handout is pride, you could make sure you include something about how wonderful you are in every conversation. During the five minutes, you are free to wander about the room, but you must**

LEADER TIP for The Study

Whenever groups discuss a list of questions, write the questions on newsprint, and tape the newsprint to the wall so groups can discuss the questions at their own pace.

interact with everyone in the group at least once. Your actions should reflect the behavior described on your piece of paper. Do not show anyone your paper or tell anyone your behavior. Ready? Go.

After five minutes, say: **Time's up.** Have kids form groups of four. Make sure each group has a person whose behavior was love, one person whose behavior was anger, one person whose behavior was pride, and one person whose behavior was encouragement. Have groups discuss the following questions:

● **Paraphrase the Scripture you looked up. What did it have to do with your behavior?**
● **How did others react to your behavior?**
● **How would this behavior affect a friendship?**
● **Do you see or exhibit any of these characteristics in your friendships?**
● **How do you usually respond to these characteristics in your friends?**

Say: **Whether we like it or not, the behavior of our friends affects us. If we hang out with cynical people, we may find ourselves responding to things in a cynical way. If we hang out with angry people, we'll probably find that their anger affects us. We need to choose our friends wisely because our friends shape who we become.**

—1 Corinthians 15:33

BIBLE EXPLORATION ▼

Famous Friends (15 to 20 minutes)

Tape four sheets of newsprint to the wall, and put markers on a nearby table. Write "fun" at the top of the first sheet, "talented" on the second, "dangerous" on the third, and "immoral" on the fourth. Point to the first sheet and say: **On this sheet of newsprint, we're going to create a list of the most fun people in the world. Each of you may add one name to the list. The person you know may be a friend, a celebrity, or an acquaintance. Use the markers I've provided.**

On the second sheet of newsprint, I'd like you to write the name of the most talented person you can think of. On the third sheet, I'd like you to list the most dangerous person you can think of. On the fourth sheet, write the name of the most immoral person you can think of.

When kids have finished, have them form four teams. Assign one of the lists to each team. Say: **I'd like you to discuss with your team how the people on your list might influence your behavior. Would your life be different if these people were your friends? How would it be different? Beside every name on your list, write the reasons you would or would not want this person as your friend. At the top of the sheet, describe how hanging out with the people on the list could change you. If you aren't familiar with a name, skip it.**

Give kids about five minutes to make their lists; then have each group share what it discovered. Ask a volunteer to read Proverbs 13:20 aloud. Then ask:

● **If the people on your sheet were your closest friends, how might they influence your behavior?**

● **Do your friends have any influence over your actions, behavior, and decisions? Explain.**

Have a volunteer read 1 Corinthians 15:33-34 aloud. Ask:

DEPTHFINDER: AVOIDING THE FORTRESS MENTALITY

High school can be a lonely, alienating time for many kids. While teenagers should be careful in their choice of friends, they can also be valuable assets and catalysts for positive change in the lives of others. Scripture admonishes us to reach out to the hurting and the downcast. We need others who will support us in our faith, but we must also avoid isolating ourselves from people who desperately need God. Christ has called us to love not only those who love us but also those who seem unlovable.

Help your students understand that the danger is not found in simply spending time with non-Christians. The danger lies in being influenced by their negative behavior. Remind kids that it is their responsibility to lead the way as witnesses for Christ.

A Friend Indeed

- How have you experienced the influence described in these verses in your own life?
- Have you ever seen it in others' lives? Explain.
- Have you ever been a positive influence in your friendships? Explain.
- What differences exist between friendships in which people are negatively influenced by others and friendships in which people influence others in a positive way?

Say: **We are all influenced by the people we spend time with. It's important that <u>we choose our friends wisely</u> to avoid being changed in a negative way. There is nothing wrong with reaching out in friendship to those who need God's love. But we need to make sure that our friendships don't affect and shape our lives in a negative way.**

"If you have five people you can call your friends, you're fortunate."

Arsenio Hall

(USA Weekend, February 1997)

A Friend Indeed 20

PERSONAL EVALUATION ▼

Your Friends (10 to 15 minutes) Give each group a sheet of paper and a pen. Say: **With your team, I want you to make a list of characteristics or attributes that are important to consider when choosing friends. Begin by reading Romans 16:17-18. See how many characteristics you can list.**

After five minutes, have each team share its characteristics. Give each teenager a sheet of paper and a pen.

Say: **Now take three minutes to list five of your current friends and evaluate how each of them fits our lists of characteristics.**

After three minutes say: **Share with a partner on your team what you've discovered about your choice of friends. Then pray with your partner for God's direction in your friendships. Ask God to help you choose your friends wisely.**

LEADER TIP for Your Friends

Be on the lookout for kids who don't have many friends. They may need encouragement to seek out godly friends and to examine what keeps them from having friendships.

ACTIVE CLOSING ▼

Up and Down (10 to 15 minutes) Say: **Find a partner who is the same gender and roughly the same size as you. Face each other, and lock arms with your partner. One of you should kneel on the floor.** Pause while students kneel. **The object of this game is to bring your partner to where you are. If you are kneeling, you will try to pull your partner down. If you are standing, you will try to pull your partner up. You may not jerk on your partner's arms; you must gradually pull harder. You must keep your feet or knees in the same location at all times. You may not let go of your partner unless one of you calls "stop." If either of you yells "stop," you both**

LEADER TIP for Up and Down

If you have time, allow students to try the game several times to see the effects of fatigue on their abilities.

DEPTH FINDER — CIRCLE OF FRIENDS

Everyone wants to be liked. And teenagers put a tremendous amount of importance on having a large group of friends. However, to sustain many friendships, individuals often compromise who they are or avoid letting others really get to know them.

Christians sometimes draw parallels between Jesus' relationships and the types of friendships we can reasonably support. We can have only one best friend (as Jesus had in John); a few intimate friends (as Jesus shared intimate aspects of his ministry with Peter, James, and John); and a dozen good friends (as Jesus had in the twelve disciples).

While the Bible never says that Jesus' relationships were a formula for friendship, they do demonstrate that no one can be everyone's friend. Encourage your students to be especially careful about the people they choose to have in their inner circles of friends, and challenge them to avoid expecting or even striving to have *everyone* like them.

A Friend Indeed 21

LEADER TIP for Up and Down

Be sure to carefully monitor kids' behavior for safety. If you have an adult-to-student ratio that's greater than ten to one, you may want to select a few students to perform this activity as a demonstration.

must let go immediately. You will have one minute to accomplish your goal.

After one minute, ask:
- Was it easier to pull someone down or pull someone up?
- How is this like friendship? different?
- What effect did strength have on the outcome? How is this like and unlike friendship?
- How do you establish and find friends who will pull you up? who you can pull up?
- How would the game be different if the person on the ground wanted to come up? if the person standing was tired or weak or wanted to come down?
- How is that like friendship?

Say: **God wants us to reach out to hurting people. He wants us to help those who need help up. But no matter how strong we are in our faith, it's possible that others can pull us down. God can give you the strength to stand, but it's important to choose your friends wisely.** Ask God to show you which relationships you should and shouldn't be in.

DEPTH FINDER — LOOKS CAN BE DECEIVING

The things that may seem pleasing at a certain time may end up being a curse. When Abram and Lot had to separate because of the size of their flocks, Abram gave Lot the choice of where to live. Lot chose what was most pleasing to his eye, the terrain with the greenest grass. However, this choice placed Lot very close to Sodom, the wicked city that was later destroyed by God's wrath.

Just as Lot was given a choice, God allows us to choose our friends. Encourage kids to pray about this choice, as they may otherwise unwittingly make choices that bring them close to destruction.

A Friend Indeed

Behavior
[BEHAVIOR]

Photocopy and cut apart the sections of this handout.
Make sure that each student in your group gets one section.

....

BEHAVIOR: *Love*

✘ Read Proverbs 17:17. What does this verse say about friendship?
✘ Demonstrate love to those around you by showing interest in their conversation and giving hugs.

....

BEHAVIOR: Anger

✘ Read Proverbs 15:1. What does this verse say about friendship?
✘ Show anger to those around you by being temperamental, aggressive, and curt.

....

BEHAVIOR: Pride

✘ Read Proverbs 16:18. What does this verse say about friendship?
✘ Brag about and concentrate on yourself in every conversation.

....

BEHAVIOR: Encouragement

✘ Read Romans 15:2. What does this verse say about friendship?
✘ Ask others how they are doing and make an effort to point out their strengths.

....

Permission to photocopy this handout from Group's Core Belief Bible Study Series granted for local church use.
Copyright © Group Publishing, Inc., P.O. Box 481, Loveland, CO 80539.

THE ISSUE: Trust

Trust Me

Helping Kids Become Trustworthy

BY MATT DIRKS

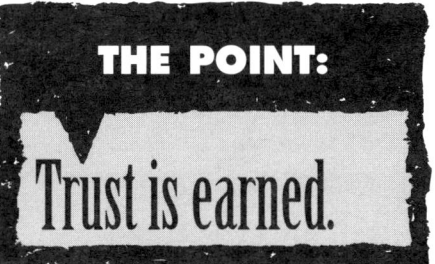

THE POINT:
Trust is earned.

■ You're only human. So it's likely you've let other people down from time to time. Maybe it was when a delicious morsel of gossip about a close friend slipped out of your mouth. Maybe it was when you completely flaked out on an important commitment you had made to your boss. Whatever the situation was, you broke someone's trust. You were seen as untrustworthy. And you probably felt horrible about your mistake. ■ Many teenagers don't feel trusted. They are denied privileges by their parents, unable to leave their campuses at lunch, and watched closely by convenience-store clerks. People generally rise—or fall—to the level of expectations others have of them. Is it any surprise that some teenagers grow up unable to trust themselves or others? ■ Use this study to help your kids take steps to end this cycle of mistrust. Challenge them to proactively build trust with others. And teach them to develop the biblical characteristics that make them trustworthy individuals.

The Study
AT A GLANCE

SECTION	MINUTES	WHAT STUDENTS WILL DO	SUPPLIES
Opening Experience	10 to 15	EARNING YOUR TRUST—Choose whether or not to trust a partner in feeding them unknown foods.	Blindfolds, plastic spoons, small paper cups, applesauce, pudding, baby food
Culture Connection	10 to 15	MODELS OF TRUST AND MISTRUST—Think of famous people who are trustworthy or untrustworthy.	Newsprint, tape, markers
Bible Connection	15 to 20	WHY WE SHOULD BE TRUSTWORTHY—Create "living sculptures" of biblical and modern stories of trust.	Bibles
Commitment	10 to 15	BECOMING TRUSTWORTHY PEOPLE—Discuss the ways they have been untrustworthy and make a decree to be trustworthy from this point on.	"Decree of Trust" handouts (p. 33), pens, candles, matches, wax paper, rubber stamp

notes:

THE POINT OF "TRUST ME":

Trust is earned.

THE BIBLE CONNECTION

GENESIS 22:1-19   God commands Abraham to sacrifice his son Isaac. Abraham trusts God and intends to obey, while Isaac trusts his father to do God's will.

GENESIS 27:1-29   Jacob deceives his father into giving him the blessing intended for his older brother, Esau.

In this study, students will choose whether to trust each other. Students will have the chance to think of people who characterize integrity and people who don't, then discover the qualities that make someone trustworthy or untrustworthy. They will look at the lives of trustworthy and untrustworthy biblical characters, then commit to taking one practical step toward becoming more trustworthy.

Through this experience, students can discover that trust is earned while being challenged to become more trustworthy.

Take time to prayerfully study the verses in The Bible Connection; then explore the information in the Depthfinder boxes throughout the study to gain a deeper understanding of how these Scripture passages connect with your young people.

BEFORE THE STUDY

For the "Earning Your Trust" activity, prepare small paper cups of applesauce, pudding, and baby food. Prepare one cup of each kind of food for every pair.

For "Becoming Trustworthy People," make one copy on parchment paper of the "Decree of Trust" (p. 33) handout for each student.

LEADER TIP for The Study

Because this topic can be so powerful and relevant to kids' lives, your group members may be tempted to get caught up in issues and lose sight of the deeper biblical principle found in The Point. Help your kids grasp The Point by guiding kids to focus on the biblical investigation and discussing how God's truth connects with reality in their lives.

THE STUDY

OPENING EXPERIENCE ▼

Earning Your Trust (10 to 15 minutes)

Have students form pairs. Have one person in each pair put on a blindfold. Give each pair two plastic spoons and three of the cups you prepared before the study.

Say: **This is a test of your trust. The people who are blindfolded must eat two of the items in the paper cups. Some of the food might be pretty good, but some of it might be pretty gross. You have two choices: You can either trust your partner and allow him or her to choose which two foods you'll eat, or you can take off your blindfold and choose for yourself. Before you make your choice, remember that <u>trust is earned.</u>**

Give the students time to make their decisions and eat the food. Then have the pairs switch the blindfold and repeat the process. Say: **Now the other person has the chance to trust or not to trust. If you were blindfolded before, you now have the chance to reward your partner's loyalty, or you have the chance to get back at him or her for feeding you something gross. Those of you who are blindfolded have the same choice: to trust or not to trust. Choose now!**

Allow time for the students to choose and eat. Bring the group back together to discuss these questions:
● **How did you feel when you had to choose to trust or not trust?**
● **Why did you choose to trust or not to trust your partner?**
● **What was the outcome of your choice?**
● **How is this similar to or different from the experiences you've had with trust in real life?**
● **With a partner, share a time your trust was broken.**

LEADER TIP for Earning Your Trust

While students are blindfolded, ask them if they are allergic to any of the foods you are having them eat. If someone reveals an allergy, make certain the student isn't fed that food.

LEADER TIP for The Study

Whenever groups discuss a list of questions, write the questions on newsprint, and tape the newsprint to the wall so groups can discuss the questions at their own pace.

DEPTH FINDER — UNDERSTANDING THE BIBLE—ABRAHAM

At first, Abraham had laughed. "A son? By Sarah? At ninety years old?" The promise from God was unbelievable. But now he stood over his bound-up son Isaac, the one whose descendants were to be more numerous than the stars in the sky.

Abraham proved himself trustworthy because he put his trust in God. Against every impulse in his body, he followed God's command to sacrifice his son and seemingly destroy the vast heritage he was to originate. And Genesis suggests that Isaac put up no resistance. He trusted his father completely, knowing that Abraham was ultimately doing only what the Lord desired.

Because of his trust and obedience, Abraham was trusted with an incredible blessing. He was made the father of the nation Israel, and Jesus entered the world through Abraham's line.

DEPTH FINDER: UNDERSTANDING YOUR STUDENTS—HOW TRUSTWORTHY ARE THEY?

While crime rates may be dropping in many parts of America, this does not seem to reflect a sudden outbreak of integrity. In the daily challenges that most students face, they are increasingly choosing to lie to get what they want. According to a recent survey, 66 percent of church kids surveyed had lied to a parent, teacher, or other older person in the last three months; and 59 percent had lied to a friend or peer. Thirty-six percent had cheated on an exam, and 15 percent had stolen money or other material possessions. And those are the kids who should know better!

For years, it has been communicated to our young people through television, movies, and even the actions of people they respect that honesty is not always the best policy. As a result, 38 percent of the church kids surveyed believe that lying might sometimes be necessary. As a leader of youth, take a look at your own life. How often do you exaggerate a story to make it more exciting? How many times have you fudged to avoid an uncomfortable situation? Those of us who help mold these impressionable young hearts must be certain that we are constantly living by the standards that we expect of them.

CULTURE CONNECTION ▼

Models of Trust and Mistrust (10 to 15 minutes)

Draw a line down the middle of a sheet of newsprint, and tape the sheet to the wall. On the top left side of the sheet, write "untrustworthy." On the right side, write "trustworthy." Give each student a marker.

Say: **I want you to think of famous people you view as trustworthy or untrustworthy. You can think of movie stars, singers, politicians, or any other celebrity. The only rule is that these people must be living. Write their names under the proper heading on this sheet, according to whether you feel you can trust them.**

Give students about five minutes to create a list of trustworthy and untrustworthy people. For each celebrity listed, ask the student who wrote the name why he or she thought of that person. Have the group vote on who is the most trustworthy and who is the least trustworthy.

Ask:
- **How do you know these people are trustworthy or untrustworthy when you've never even met them?**
- **What are the characteristics of a trustworthy person? an untrustworthy person?**
- **What would have to happen before you would move the names of some of the people on the left side of the sheet to the right side? people on the right side of the sheet to the left side?**
- **How important is it to you that your heroes be trustworthy? your friends?**
- **What is it like to have a relationship with a person you don't trust?**
- **How have *you* earned the trust of your friends?**

Trust Me

BIBLE CONNECTION ▼

Why We Should Be Trustworthy
(15 to 20 minutes)

Say: **There was a character in the Bible who trusted others completely. Sometimes he was rewarded for his trust, and sometimes he wasn't. Two people he trusted fell on opposite ends of the trust scale. One was completely trustworthy; the other was completely untrustworthy. The character I'm talking about is Isaac. He trusted his father, Abraham, and his son Jacob.**

Form two teams of equal size. Assign Genesis 22:1-19 to one team and Genesis 27:1-29 to the other. Have each team read its assigned passage aloud by having each person read one or two verses. Then direct each team to create two "living sculptures."

Say: **A living sculpture is a freeze-frame glimpse of a part of a story. Every member of your team must be involved in your living sculpture. You might be a character or a tree, or a few of you might form a mountain. You may also use chairs or anything else in the room as part of your sculpture. Remember to create a single moment in your living sculpture. For example, if you create a sculpture of Abraham tying Isaac to the altar, a few people could act as the altar by getting on their hands and knees, another person could lie across their backs, and another could act as if he or she is fastening the ropes. Remember that you aren't going to act the scene out; you're just showing one freeze-frame moment.**

Your first sculpture will demonstrate a scene from the Bible story. Show the scene that your group thinks demonstrates the strongest instance of trust in the story. Your second sculpture will portray a modern-day situation that is similar to the Bible story. For example, you might create a living sculpture of a pickpocket to demonstrate how Jacob robbed Esau of his birthright.

Give kids five or ten minutes; then have one team present its first sculpture while the other team tries to interpret it. Then have the team create and explain the sculpture of a modern-day event. Have the second team present its sculptures in the same way.

DEPTHFINDER — **UNDERSTANDING YOUR STUDENTS— TRAINED TO MISTRUST**

While their parents probably grew up leaving their doors unlocked, today's high school students were born into a world in which they couldn't talk to strangers, couldn't go out after dark, and couldn't eat the unwrapped candy in their Halloween baskets. Large numbers of them were abused or neglected as children. Why should we be surprised if they have trouble trusting other people?

According to a recent survey, 32 percent of churched youth in America would say that they usually mistrust people, and 33 percent would say they are generally skeptical. For students to display the kind of loving trust God desires of them, they must learn to separate healthy caution toward the outside world from unhealthy mistrust and cynicism toward everything and everyone they come in contact with.

Then ask:
- Why did you choose those scenes as the strongest instances of trust in the Bible stories?
- Why do you think Isaac trusted Abraham?
- If you were in Isaac's shoes, would you have trusted Abraham?
- Why do you think Jacob trusted his mother?
- Do you think Jacob earned Isaac's trust? Explain.
- What are some ways trust and mistrust appear in the world? in your life?
- Who in these stories do you most want to be like? Why?

COMMITMENT ▼

Becoming Trustworthy People (10 to 15 minutes)

Have students return to their pairs from the first activity. Have each pair discuss these questions:
- Do you feel that people generally trust you? Why or why not?
- What's one thing you've done to break someone's trust?
- Have you been able to regain that person's trust? Explain.
- If not, what do you need to do to regain your integrity in this person's eyes?

Give each student a copy of the "Decree of Trust" handout (p. 33) and a pen. Have teenagers answer the following question by discussing it with their partners and then writing their answers on the handout:
- What is one practical step you could take to be more trustworthy?

Say: **In ancient times, kings made lots of decrees. Decrees were statements that became laws. If the king wanted it done, it would be done. Kings would write down their decrees on pieces of**

LEADER TIP for Becoming Trustworthy People

If you have a high level of trust with your students, have kids form groups of four, and give each group a candle and matches. Make sure you have a fire extinguisher on hand in case of an accident.

DEPTHFINDER: UNDERSTANDING YOUR STUDENTS—DEVELOPING TRUST IN THE LITTLE THINGS

High schoolers are used to being mistrusted. They might feel that there is nothing they can do to make their parents, teachers, or other adults fully trust them. They feel ready to take on new privileges, but they often don't know how to prove that they are capable of assuming new responsibilities.

Teenagers need to know that the privileges they seek will come when people see their trustworthy character. And they need to understand that developing a trustworthy character that lasts through the big things in life starts with the little things at home. Challenge students to follow through with and even go beyond their responsibilities and commitments to their families. Dare them to "over-obey" their parents by doing things around the house that they weren't even told to do, such as mowing the lawn before they're asked or doing the dishes when it's not their turn. When students prove themselves trustworthy in these little things, the larger privileges they seek will usually follow!

parchment, then the decrees would be sealed with pieces of wax imprinted with the king's seal. This way, everyone would know that the documents could be trusted. We're going to do the same thing today. You've just made a decree, and it should be one that you intend to keep. So we're going to seal it.

Have each student roll up his or her parchment. Light a candle, and assist each student in sealing his or her decree. Spread out a sheet of wax paper. Over the waxed paper, tip the candle so that the wax drips onto the rolled-up parchment. While the wax is still soft, imprint it with a rubber stamp. Encourage your students to take as much responsibility in this process as you feel comfortable giving them.

Say: **Let's close in silent prayer. As you pray, ask God to help you earn the trust of others. Ask for God's forgiveness for the times you've broken others' trust. And ask God to point out times in your life when you have not acted with integrity.**

After a few minutes, close the prayer by saying: **In Jesus' name. Amen.**

"But the angel of the Lord called out to him from heaven, 'Abraham! Abraham!' 'Here I am,' he replied. 'Do not lay a hand on the boy,' he said, 'Do not do anything to him. Now I know that you fear God, because you have not withheld from me your son, your only son.'"

—Genesis 22:11-12

Decree of Trust

I, _____,
hereby decree that in order to maintain
my trustworthy character,
from this day forward I will...

THE ISSUE: Dating

Teenage Romance
The Truth About Lasting Relationships

by Amy Nappa

■ "I almost totally clam up...then I end up in completely meaningless conversations...that have a lot of nervous energy, and I usually end up complaining about something or other. I tend to start rubbing my shoulders, too...they get real tense..." ■ If this sounds like a teenager's thoughts on visiting a dying relative, guess again. This is the start of a high school romance as described on America Online. ■ So much of a teenager's life revolves around relationships, especially those with the opposite gender. But what's the purpose of these relationships? Where do they lead? And how will they end? ■ This study takes kids through the stages of dating relationships and helps them evaluate God's perspective on the work and commitment required to make their relationships last.

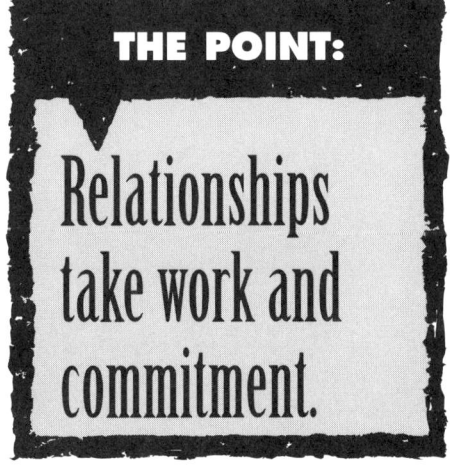

THE POINT:
Relationships take work and commitment.

The Study
AT A GLANCE

SECTION	MINUTES	WHAT STUDENTS WILL DO	SUPPLIES
Dating Simulation	10 to 15	FIRST DATE—Role play the beginning of a new relationship.	Prepared envelopes and index cards
	10 to 15	FIRST FIGHT—Evaluate their relationships based on new information.	Prepared index cards
	10 to 15	ADVICE FROM ANOTHER COUPLE—Study and discuss Mary and Joseph's relationship.	Bibles
Breaking Up	5 to 10	YES, IT'S OVER—End their model relationships with prayer.	
Personal Application	5 to 10	MOVING ON—Determine how to apply their model relationships to real life.	

notes:

THE POINT OF "TEENAGE ROMANCE":

Relationships take work and commitment.

THE BIBLE CONNECTION

MATTHEW 1:18-25 and LUKE 1:26-38; 2:1-21 — These passages describe how Mary and Joseph stayed together through difficult circumstances.

In this study, kids will compare simulated and actual relationships to the relationship of Mary and Joseph.

Through this comparison, kids can see that a lasting relationship involves work and commitment, even when situations change and the relationship seems doomed.

Explore the verses in The Bible Connection; then examine the information in the Depthfinder boxes throughout the study to gain a deeper understanding of how these Scriptures connect with your young people.

BEFORE THE STUDY

For the "First Date" activity, gather one index card and one envelope for every two students. On the outside of each envelope, write one of the following phrases:
- Physical Attraction
- Common Interest
- Convenience

Also title one envelope "Parent Sets You Up."

Set out one index card to correspond with each envelope. Use the following suggestions to complete each card:
- On a "Physical Attraction" card, you could write, "Someone better looking comes along."
- On a "Common Interest" card, you could write, "One of you takes up a new hobby."
- On a "Convenience" card, you could write, "Someone better comes along" or "Your situation changes, and it's no longer convenient to be together."
- On the "Parent Sets You Up" card, write, "Girlfriend becomes pregnant by another guy."

Place each card in its corresponding envelope, then seal the envelopes.

LEADER TIP for The Study

Because this topic can be so powerful and relevant to kids' lives, your group members may be tempted to get caught up in issues and lose sight of the deeper biblical principle found in The Point. Help your kids grasp The Point by guiding kids to focus on the biblical investigation and discussing how God's truth connects with reality in their lives.

Teenage Romance 37

THE STUDY

DATING SIMULATION ▼

First Date (10 to 15 minutes)

Once everyone has arrived, separate the guys from the girls. Since the focus of the study is dating relationships, your goal is to form as many male/female pairs as possible. However, since it's unlikely that your group will have an equal number of guys and girls, some mixed-gender trios may be necessary. Try not to form any same-gender pairs or trios if at all possible.

Say: **Today we'll be learning about <u>the work and commitment involved in relationships</u>, especially dating relationships. For the rest of our time together, consider your partner** (partners) **to be your boyfriend or girlfriend. If you're in a trio, consider yourself part of a dating triangle.**

Relationships, especially at the beginning, are usually based on something like a common interest, physical attraction, or even convenience. I'm going to assign each group a relational basis.

Give each pair or trio one of the envelopes. Kids may read the outside of the envelopes, but don't let them open them yet. Be sure one male/female pair gets the "Parent Sets You Up" envelope. (If you have any same-gender trios, give them a "Common Interest" or "Convenience" envelope.)

Then say: **With your partner(s), define your relationship based on the information written on your envelope. For example, if**

> **LEADER TIP for Dating Simulation**
>
> If you are forced to form one or more same-gender pairs or trios, make it clear to the class that the kids in those pairs or trios are *not* simulating dating relationships. Instead have them simulate a friendship and modify your explanations throughout the study to include friend-to-friend relationships.

> **LEADER TIP for Dating Simulation**
>
> Be sensitive to the relationships in your group. If a guy and a girl in your group are dating each other, think carefully about how this exercise could affect their relationship. If you think the activity would only provide opportunity for reinforcement of negative attitudes, separate the couple. However, if you think the activity would give the couple a healthier view of dating each other, make sure they are paired together.

DEPTH FINDER — UNDERSTANDING THESE KIDS

If the young people in your group are anything like ten thousand other kids nationwide, here are the top ten things that turn them off on a date:

TOP TEN TURNOFFS:

1. Looks
2. Negative personality
3. Bad manners
4. Body odor
5. Bad breath
6. Sexual pressure
7. Other
8. Smoking
9. Talking too much
10. Using drugs

(Taken from a national youth survey as reported in GROUP Magazine, November/December 1994)

Teenage Romance 38

DEPTH FINDER: UNDERSTANDING THESE KIDS

While this study focuses on the work and commitment required to maintain a relationship, not every dating relationship your kids experience is supposed to last forever. In fact, sometimes ending a dating relationship can be the wisest choice a young person can make. Here's what one sixteen-year-old girl said about ending a relationship, as recorded in the book *Ask Me If I Care* by Nancy J. Rubin:

"Breaking up is such a return of energy after three years. It's almost too exciting. I'm really thankful…Suddenly I'm remembering all those things I like to do, remembering new sensations of excitement, relief,…release, and a life-loving, pervasive positiveness toward the whole experience."

As you lead this study, avoid inadvertently pushing your kids to begin serious relationships with members of the opposite sex. Instead, use this study to encourage kids to see the value of dating a variety of people without becoming seriously attached to anyone until later.

you have a "Common Interest" envelope, decide what your common interest will be. Make sure it's a common interest you really share; don't make something up. If your relationship is based on physical attraction, say what you find attractive in each other. If your parents set you up, say what you think they saw in this other person that made them want you to date him or her. If yours is a relationship of convenience, tell your partner what you like about him or her that makes you willing to date or hang out together. Remember, you're just starting a relationship here, so you want to make all of your comments positive ones!

Allow two minutes for partners to discuss and affirm what is positive about each other and their relationship. Then call time.

First Fight (10 to 15 minutes)

When pairs have finished their discussions, say: **It's time for your first fight! Open your envelope to find out what has just changed in your relationship.**

After kids have opened their envelopes, say: **Now you must renegotiate your relationship based on this new information. Be honest with each other as you try to work out the problem. For example, if you just found out that your boyfriend broke his nose, would you honestly still find him attractive? Or could you overlook this temporary disfigurement? Discuss your assigned situation with your partner, and decide if you can work things out or if you'll have to break up or end your friendship.**

After two minutes, end the discussion, and see if any pairs decided to end their relationships. If so, have them form new pairs (or trios) with other available persons. If only one pair wants to call it quits, they'll have to stay together out of convenience. After any changes have been made, continue the study.

LEADER TIP for Dating Simulation

If you have kids in mixed-gender trios, have them go through the "Dating Simulation" activities as a "love triangle," in which the one girl (or guy) is dating both of the other two trio members at the same time. That will allow kids to discuss their feelings about people who pursue more than one dating relationship at once.

Teenage Romance 39

Advice From Another Couple (10 to 15 minutes)

Say: **Lots of times when couples fight, they ask the people they trust for advice. Let's see what advice on relationships we can get from a couple in the Bible.**

Each dating pair or trio will need a Bible. Assign each group one of the following passages to read together: Matthew 1:18-25; Luke 1:26-38; or Luke 2:1-21.

Say: **Read your passage; then summarize it in your own words. As you study your passage, look for ways Mary and Joseph demonstrated that <u>relationships take work and commitment</u>.**

After students have done this, have each pair or trio join with two other groups that had different passages. Have kids tell one another what they discovered from their assigned passages. Then have kids discuss these questions in their groups:

● **What was the basis of Mary and Joseph's relationship?**
● **Why do you think God allowed them to have problems in their relationship?**
● **How did they respond?**
● **What kept them together?**
● **Do you think Mary and Joseph believed that <u>relationships take work and commitment</u>? Why or why not?**
● **Do you believe that's true for your own dating relationship?**

DEPTHFINDER: THE BETROTHAL SYSTEM

Mary and Joseph weren't just "engaged" in the sense we know it today; they were "betrothed" to each other.

What's the difference?

During Mary and Joseph's time, Hebrew families typically arranged their children's marriages. This arrangement was sealed with a legally binding contract between the families involved. Once the children reached their early teenage years, they were officially "betrothed." From then on they were considered married and were called husband and wife, even though each person continued to live with his or her own family. This living situation continued for one year to prove the sexual purity of the bride. (In other words, if she became pregnant during this time, she obviously wasn't sexually pure.) After a year, the husband would go to his wife's home and claim his bride. They would then live together and physically consummate their marriage.

When Luke refers to Mary and Joseph's engagement, he is saying the couple was in this one-year betrothal period. When Mary became pregnant, Joseph could have legally divorced her. However, he took her into his home earlier than the custom allowed but did not consummate their marriage physically until after the year was up. It's likely that Joseph's decision evoked a great deal of gossip and ridicule from the townsfolk, but Mary and Joseph both knew the truth and chose to withstand the pressures of their culture.

Permission to photocopy this Depthfinder from Group's Core Belief Bible Study Series granted for local church use. Copyright © Group Publishing, Inc., P.O. Box 481, Loveland, CO 80539.

Teenage Romance   40

Why or why not?

Call everyone back together, and ask the pair who had the "Parent Sets You Up" envelope to talk about their situation and how they resolved (or didn't resolve) it. Then ask:

- **How is this pair's situation like or unlike that of Mary and Joseph?**
- **What advice do you think Mary or Joseph would give each of you in your relationship today?**
- **Do you think people give up on relationships too easily in our culture? Why or why not?**
- **Do you think dating should even be a part of your high school experience? Why or why not?**
- **What kind of work and commitment is necessary to keep a dating relationship going?**
- **What kind of commitment is necessary to allow a dating relationship to end peacefully?**

Say: **Let's explore that last question more deeply.**

> "Let us therefore make every effort to do what leads to peace and to mutual edification."
>
> —Romans 14:19

LEADER TIP for Breaking Up

If kids balk at the idea of praying with a boyfriend or girlfriend at the end of a relationship, take a moment to help them examine their opinions more closely. Ask:

- Why would it be hard to pray with your partner at the end of the relationship?
- If you did pray together, what would you pray for the other person?
- How could praying for the other person help you handle the breakup more easily?

BREAKING UP ▼

Yes, It's Over (5 to 10 minutes)

Have kids return to their dating partners. Then say: **All serious relationships take work and commitment.** But that doesn't mean every dating relationship is supposed to last forever. When it's time for a relationship to end, what's the best way to go about ending it? Tell your partner(s) the ideal way you'd like someone to tell you that your relationship is over.

After kids have shared, say: **It's time for your "relationship" to end. Now that you know the kindest way to break up with your partner, go ahead and do it. Take turns, be gentle, and remember to tell your partner at least one thing you've appreciated about sharing this relationship with him or her.**

After kids "break up," say: **I'd like each pair or trio here to "close the book" on your model relationship in a unique way—by praying together. Thank God for what you've gotten to know about your partner(s), and pray for each other's future relationships.**

> "Don't let anyone look down on you because you are young, but set an example for the believers in speech, in life, in love, in faith and in purity."
>
> —1 TIMOTHY 4:12

PERSONAL APPLICATION ▼

Moving On (5 to 10 minutes)
Have kids form a circle and join hands. Say: **The relationships we experienced today were temporary. We're all still friends, but these model relationships are over.** Ask:
● **How were these relationships like or unlike real relationships?**
● **What did you learn about the work and commitment involved in relationships?**
● **How can what you've learned help you in relationships now and in the future?**

Close with a group hug.

DEPTH FINDER — ARRANGED MARRIAGES BACK IN VOGUE?

What's your reaction to this statement?

"The Bible doesn't endorse dating; in fact, arranged marriages are what God intended."

Sound a bit extreme? Well, an article supporting this belief recently appeared in Patriarch, a Christian men's magazine. Among other things, the article stated:

● Dating is a temporary romantic relationship that's designed to eventually end. Thus it teaches us more about divorce than it does about marriage.

● When the Bible says to love your husband or wife, that means to love the one you are married to. It doesn't mean to marry the one you love.

● Dating encourages people to form emotional bonds without permanent commitment. That means you become emotionally close to someone without the security of knowing he or she will be in this relationship with you permanently.

THE ISSUE: Sexual Abstinence

Sex Worth Waiting For
Learning to Treasure God's Powerful Gift

BY LINDA SNYDER

■ Right now, about half of teenagers are doing it. ■ Of those, one out of six will catch a sexually transmitted disease this year. One out of ten of girls will get pregnant. And about 40 percent of those who do will get an abortion. ■ But even among those who miss the diseases and the unwanted pregnancies, there is one cost they cannot avoid: a shattered heart. ■ Our sex-saturated society devalues and distorts one of God's greatest gifts. And many teenagers have bought into the lie. They don't see their sexuality in all its God-given splendor; instead, they've settled for a cheaper version of "true love." And that choice is killing them, one night at a time. ■ This study exposes kids to a powerful picture of positive and healthy sexuality surrounded by respect, dignity, longevity, and exclusivity. It's "good sex," God's way.

THE POINT:

Sex creates a bond that thrives only in marriage.

The Study
AT A GLANCE

SECTION	MINUTES	WHAT STUDENTS WILL DO	SUPPLIES
Warm Up	up to 5	BATTING PRACTICE—Choose words that describe their comfort levels when talking about sex.	Pencils, index cards
Taking the Field	12 to 15	FIRST BASE—Choose words that define "good sex."	Newsprint, tape, markers
	12 to 15	SECOND BASE—Form teams to search the Bible for the answer to the question "What is sex for?"	Bibles, index cards, pencils
	12 to 15	THIRD BASE—Use a target to explain the environment in which sex thrives best.	Newsprint, tape, marker
Final Run	5 to 10	FOUL PLAY—Try to peel apart glued paper hearts without tearing the paper.	Construction paper, white glue, pencils

notes:

THE POINT OF "SEX WORTH WAITING FOR":

Sex creates a bond that thrives only in marriage.

THE BIBLE CONNECTION

PROVERBS 5:3-8, 15-17	Solomon warns his sons not to have sex outside of marriage.
SONG OF SONGS 4:1-7; 5:10-16	The man and woman in the story express how attracted they are to each other.
SONG OF SONGS 8:6-7	The man in the story describes the amazing power of true love.
1 CORINTHIANS 6:18-20	Paul instructs Christians to flee from sexual immorality.
1 THESSALONIANS 4:3-8	Paul admonishes Christians to avoid sexual sin.

In this study, kids will conduct a three-way investigation to answer the question "What is sex for?"

By exploring the Bible's answer to this question and creating a new definition of "good sex," your kids can discover why sex before marriage is destructive and recognize their own need to save sex for the marriage relationship.

Explore the verses in The Bible Connection; then examine the information in the Depthfinder boxes to gain a deeper understanding of how these Scriptures connect with your young people.

LEADER TIP for The Study

Because this topic is so powerful and relevant to kids' lives, your group members may be tempted to get caught up in issues and lose sight of the deeper biblical principle found in The Point. Help your kids grasp The Point by guiding them to focus on the biblical investigation and by discussing how God's truth connects with reality in their lives.

THE STUDY

WARM UP ▼

Batting Practice (up to 5 minutes)
Give each person an index card and a pencil. Tell

kids to write on their cards one word that describes how they feel when talking about sex. Provide examples of "feeling" words such as "uncomfortable," "embarrassed," "silly," "confident," or "excited." Keep the responses anonymous to encourage kids to be honest.

Collect the cards, shuffle them, then ask the group to join you in prayer. Pray: **Lord, we want to learn from you today about our sexuality, but that can be difficult when confusing feelings get in the way. As we talk about this issue today, help us each deal with these emotions...**Read the cards aloud as part of your prayer, then say: **Thank you, Lord. In Jesus' name, amen.**

After the prayer, say: **Everyone has different feelings when talking about sex. As we "warm up" to the idea of sharing our feelings, remember to respect each other's ideas and listen to each other without put-downs or inappropriate humor.**

TAKING THE FIELD ▼

LEADER TIP for First Base

As the kids create their lists, be sure they understand there are no right or wrong answers. Encourage them to think of as many words as possible. The longer their lists, the clearer the word picture will be.

First Base (12 to 15 minutes)

Say: **In order to talk about sex, we must first agree on what positive or healthy sex is. Let's define positive or healthy sex by creating word lists that describe these key words: "love," "sexuality," and "respect."**

Have kids form three groups; then give each group a marker and a sheet of newsprint with one of the key words written at the top.

Say: **In your group, create a list of synonyms and related words that describe your key word. For example, for "sexuality" you might list "intimacy" or "lust." Please avoid writing down anything that others might find offensive. Go!**

When each group has listed about ten words, have kids select two words that best describe their key word and write them on a sheet of newsprint taped to the wall. When all the words have been revealed, ask:

● **What words from this list seem to be the most important for**

LEADER TIP for First Base

If your group has fewer than nine people, have kids remain in one group to create all three lists. That will allow kids to more effectively pool their creativity.

DEPTH FINDER — UNDERSTANDING THE BIBLE

As kids study the relationship between the lovers in the Song of Songs, they might be tempted to interpret that relationship as permission to have sex outside of marriage. You can help your kids understand the true meaning of these passages by explaining these facts:

● The Song of Songs describes the love between a king and a Shulammite woman. The book follows the couple through the courtship, the wedding, and the married life that follows. Although the couple is in love from the beginning of the book, they do not consummate the relationship until after they're married.

● The term "lover" used in the Song of Songs doesn't mean "sexual partner" as it might today. Instead, it's simply a term of affection like "my love" or "my beloved."

positive or healthy sex?
- Are there any words on this list that surprise you? Why or why not?
- Are there any words you would add or delete? Explain.
- How is our word picture of positive or healthy sex like or unlike the way society views sex? your classmates view sex? you view sex? God views sex?

Second Base (12 to 15 minutes)
Say: **When you have sex without considering the importance of the key words we've listed here, sex becomes cheap and your relationships end up hurting you. <u>Sex creates a bond that thrives only in marriage</u>. We'll spend the rest of the study exploring that truth.**

Say: **Now that we've decided what positive or healthy sex is about, let's see if we can answer the next question: "What is sex for?"**

LEADER TIP for Second Base

If you have more than twenty students, have the kids in each corner form pairs. This will speed up the discussion time and allow everyone to participate.

"Flee from sexual immorality. All other sins a man commits are outside his body, but he who sins sexually sins against his own body."

—1 CORINTHIANS 6:18

Sex Worth Waiting For   49

Form groups of three. Have each trio designate one person to be a one, one person to be a two, and one person to be a three. Give each person an index card, a pencil, and a Bible. Have all the ones write "Proverbs 5:3-8, 15-17" at the top of their cards. Have all the twos write "Song of Songs 4:1-7; 5:10-16; 8:6-7" at the top of their cards. Have all the threes write "1 Corinthians 6:18-20; 1 Thessalonians 4:3-8" at the top of their cards.

Assign each number a corner of the room. As soon as groups are in their respective corners, have kids work together to write the answer to this question on their cards:

● **According to your assigned Scripture passages, what is sex for?**

While groups are working, be available to help kids discover how their Scripture passages help answer the question "What is sex for?" Then, when all three sections have finished, have kids return to their trios. Starting with the ones, give each trio member one minute to teach the others what he or she learned.

"It is God's will that you should be sanctified: that you should avoid sexual immorality; that each of you should learn to control his own body in a way that is **holy and honorable."**

—1 THESSALONIANS 4:3-4

DEPTH FINDER: UNDERSTANDING THESE KIDS

Unless the kids in your class defy the odds, several of them are probably sexually active already. Because of this, at some point in the study, it's important for you to talk about God's forgiveness and the healing power of the grace of Jesus Christ.

Use the following passages to help you address the issue of forgiveness: 2 Samuel 11:1–12:13; Psalm 32; Psalm 51; Ephesians 2:1-10; and 1 John 1:9.

Then say: **In the previous activity, we created a list of words describing positive and healthy sex. Now we've looked through Scripture to figure out exactly what sex is for. Now comes the real test.**

Based on all your trio's information, write on the back of one of your cards a definition of positive and healthy sex. Your definition may not be longer than one sentence, and all three members must agree on it. You have two minutes. Go!

Some group members may have trouble agreeing on what exactly constitutes sex. Is it "making out"? foreplay? sexual intercourse? all of these? If a debate arises, it may help to read one of Webster's definitions of sex: "anything connected with sexual gratification or reproduction or the urge for these; especially, the attraction of those of one sex for those of the other."

After two minutes, have each trio read its definition to the rest of the group. Then say: **Here's one more definition for you to consider: "Positive and healthy sex occurs only when two people share intimate love, trust, and respect in an exclusive, marriage relationship."**

Repeat the definition, then ask:
● **What's your reaction to this definition?**
● **Do you believe that <u>sex creates a bond that thrives only in marriage</u>? Why or why not?**
● **How far is too far to go sexually with a boyfriend or girlfriend?**

Say: **Let's use your definitions of positive and healthy sex to decide whether sex really can thrive outside of marriage.**

Third Base (12 to 15 minutes)

Create a large version of the "Sex Target" (see diagram) on a sheet of newsprint, and tape it to a wall. One at a time, have trios read aloud their definitions of positive and healthy sex then tape them to the Sex Target where they think positive and healthy sex thrives best.

After all the trios have done this, ask:
● **What does this activity tell you about sex? about relationships?**
● **How does sex create a bond between two people?**

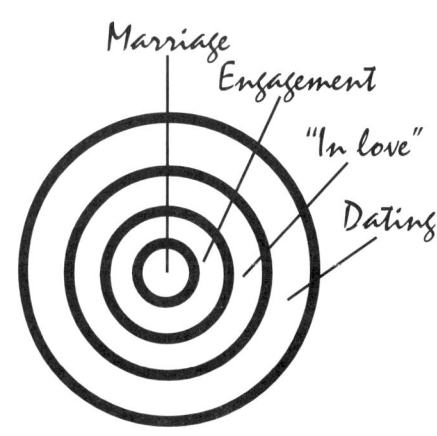

SEX TARGET

LEADER TIP for Third Base

If a group decides that sex is OK outside of marriage, ask these questions:

● Do you believe the Bible contains God's instructions for how we should live? Why or why not?

● How do you reconcile the fact that the Bible doesn't support your position on sex outside of marriage?

● How can you be certain that you're right and that God and the Bible are wrong?

● Why does the sexual bond thrive only in marriage?
● Why do you think God wants us to avoid sex outside of marriage?

Say: <u>**Sex creates a bond that thrives only in marriage.**</u> We can choose to have sex outside of marriage, but when we do, we not only disobey God, we also hurt ourselves, our future spouses, and the people we have sex with. Sex is powerful. That's why God designed it to stay within the bounds of a marriage relationship.

FINAL RUN ▼

Foul Play (5 to 10 minutes) Set out several bottles of white glue, and give each person a sheet of construction paper and a pencil. Have each person tear two heart shapes out of the construction paper and glue the shapes together. Make sure kids glue the edges of the sheet together. On each heart, have kids write one way having sex would bond them to another person. After a minute, ask volunteers to tell the group what they wrote. Then say: **Sex will create a bond, every time. God made sex to create a permanent bond between two people. Sex bonds us together just as our paper hearts are bonded together.**

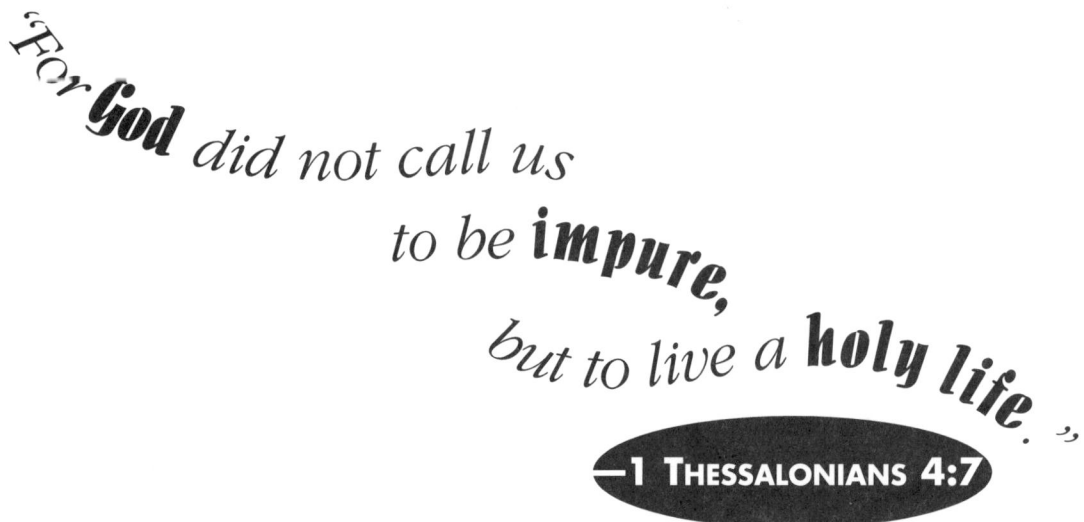

"For **God** did not call us to be **impure,** but to live a **holy life.**"
—1 THESSALONIANS 4:7

Sex Worth Waiting For 52

Have students set their paper hearts aside. Direct students to pray individually about their attitudes and desires concerning sex. Encourage students who have already had sex to pray for God's forgiveness and restoration. Challenge students who have not had sex to pray for God's strength to stand strong and for God to help their future spouses stand strong.

Have kids try to separate their two hearts without damaging them. Once all the hearts have been torn apart, say: **When we choose to have sex outside of marriage, the bond that sex creates rips us apart, sometimes even before the relationship is over. <u>Sex creates a bond that thrives only in marriage</u>. Outside of marriage, sex makes us look like this!** Hold up one of the torn paper hearts.

Say: **Take the paper heart home with you to serve as a reminder of what happens to your heart when you have sex outside of marriage. Strive for sexual and spiritual purity.**

DEPTHFINDER — UNDERSTANDING THESE KIDS

The "love rationale" so prevalent in youth culture today claims that sex is OK if two people "really love each other." But what is love? How do you define it? Love is difficult for just about anyone to define, including your young people. So how can kids know when they're really "in love"? For example, is it really love if it's based solely on emotion? Is it really love if it doesn't involve a lifetime commitment?

To help your kids gain a clear picture of what real love is all about, check out 1 Corinthians 13:1-8a. Challenge kids to compare their concepts of love with the description in that passage; then they can see how deep their "love" relationships really go.

why Active and Interactive Learning works with teenagers

Let's Start With the Big Picture

Think back to a major life lesson you've learned.
Got it? Now answer these questions:
- Did you learn your lesson from something you read?
- Did you learn it from something you heard?
- Did you learn it from something you experienced?

If you're like 99 percent of your peers, you answered "yes" only to the third question—you learned your life lesson from something you experienced.

This simple test illustrates the most convincing reason for using active and interactive learning with young people: People learn best through experience. Or to put it even more simply, people learn by doing.

Learning by doing is what active learning is all about. No more sitting quietly in chairs and listening to a speaker expound theories about God—that's passive learning. Active learning gets kids out of their chairs and into the experience of life. With active learning, kids get to *do* what they're studying. They *feel* the effects of the principles you teach. They *learn* by experiencing truth firsthand.

Active learning works because it recognizes three basic learning needs and uses them in concert to enable young people to make discoveries on their own and to find practical life applications for the truths they believe.

So what are these three basic learning needs?
1. Teenagers need action.
2. Teenagers need to think.
3. Teenagers need to talk.

Read on to find out exactly how these needs will be met by using the active and interactive learning techniques in Group's Core Belief Bible Study Series in your youth group.

1. Teenagers Need Action

Aircraft pilots know well the difference between passive and active learning. Their passive learning comes through listening to flight instructors and reading flight-instruction books. Their active learning comes

Helpful Stuff

through actually flying an airplane or flight simulator. Books and lectures may be helpful, but pilots really learn to fly by manipulating a plane's controls themselves.

We can help young people learn in a similar way. Though we may engage students passively in some reading and listening to teachers, their understanding and application of God's Word will really take off through simulated and real-life experiences.

Forms of active learning include simulation games; role-plays; service projects; experiments; research projects; group pantomimes; mock trials; construction projects; purposeful games; field trips; and, of course, the most powerful form of active learning—real-life experiences.

We can more fully explain active learning by exploring four of its characteristics:

- **Active learning is an adventure.** Passive learning is almost always predictable. Students sit passively while the teacher or speaker follows a planned outline or script.

In active learning, kids may learn lessons the teacher never envisioned. Because the leader trusts students to help create the learning experience, learners may venture into unforeseen discoveries. And often the teacher learns as much as the students.

- **Active learning is fun and captivating.** What are we communicating when we say, "OK, the fun's over—time to talk about God"? What's the hidden message? That joy is separate from God? And that learning is separate from joy?

What a shame.

Active learning is not joyless. One seventh-grader we interviewed clearly remembered her best Sunday school lesson: "Jesus was the light, and we went into a dark room and shut off the lights. We had a candle, and we learned that Jesus is the light and the dark can't shut off the light." That's active learning. Deena enjoyed the lesson. She had fun. And she learned.

Active learning intrigues people. Whether they find a foot-washing experience captivating or maybe a bit uncomfortable, they learn. And they learn on a level deeper than any work sheet or teacher's lecture could ever reach.

- **Active learning involves everyone.** Here the difference between passive and active learning becomes abundantly clear. It's like the difference between watching a football game on television and actually playing in the game.

The "trust walk" provides a good example of involving everyone in active learning. Half of the group members put on blindfolds; the other half serve as guides. The "blind" people trust the guides to lead them through the building or outdoors. The guides prevent the blind people from falling down stairs or tripping over rocks. Everyone needs to participate to learn the inherent lessons of trust, faith, doubt, fear, confidence, and servanthood. Passive spectators of this experience would learn little, but participants learn a great deal.

- **Active learning is focused through debriefing.** Activity simply for activity's sake doesn't usually result in good learning. Debriefing—evaluating an experience by discussing it in pairs or small groups—helps focus the experience and draw out its meaning. Debriefing helps sort and order the information students gather during the experience. It helps learners relate the recently experienced activity to their lives.

The process of debriefing is best started immediately after an experience. We use a three-step process in debriefing: reflection, interpretation, and application.

Reflection—This first step asks the students, "How did you feel?" Active-learning experiences typically evoke an emotional reaction, so it's appropriate to begin debriefing at that level.

Some people ask, "What do feelings have to do with education?" Feelings have everything to do with education. Think back again to that time in your life when you learned a big lesson. In all likelihood, strong feelings accompanied that lesson. Our emotions tend to cement things into our memories.

When you're debriefing, use open-ended questions to probe feelings. Avoid questions that can be answered with a "yes" or "no." Let your learners know that there are no wrong answers to these "feeling" questions. Everyone's feelings are valid.

Interpretation—The next step in the debriefing process asks, "What does this mean to you? How is this experience like or unlike some other aspect of your life?" Now you're asking people to identify a message or principle from the experience.

You want your learners to discover the message for themselves. So instead of telling students your answers, take the time to ask questions that encourage self-discovery. Use Scripture and discussion in pairs or small groups to explore how the actions and effects of the activity might translate to their lives.

Alert! Some of your people may interpret wonderful messages that you never intended. That's not failure! That's the Holy Spirit at work. God allows us to catch different glimpses of his kingdom even when we all look through the same glass.

Application—The final debriefing step asks, "What will you do about it?" This step moves learning into action. Your young people have shared a common experience. They've discovered a principle. Now they must create something new with what they've just experienced and interpreted. They must integrate the message into their lives.

The application stage of debriefing calls for a decision. Ask your students how they'll change, how they'll grow, what they'll do as a result of your time together.

2. Teenagers Need to Think

Today's students have been trained not to think. They aren't dumber than previous generations. We've simply conditioned them not to use their heads.

You see, we've trained our kids to respond with the simplistic answers they think the teacher wants to hear. Fill-in-the-blank student workbooks and teachers who ask dead-end questions such as "What's the capital of Delaware?" have produced kids and adults who have learned not to think.

And it doesn't just happen in junior high or high school. Our children are schooled very early not to think. Teachers attempt to help kids read with nonsensical fill-in-the-blank drills, word scrambles, and missing-letter puzzles.

Helping teenagers think requires a paradigm shift in how we teach. We need to plan for and set aside time for higher-order thinking and be willing to reduce our time spent on lower-order parroting. Group's Core Belief Bible Study Series is designed to help you do just that.

Thinking classrooms look quite different from traditional classrooms. In most church environments, the teacher does most of the talking and hopes that knowledge will transmit from his or her brain to the students'. In thinking settings, the teacher coaches students to ponder, wonder, imagine, and problem-solve.

3. Teenagers Need to Talk

Everyone knows that the person who learns the most in any class is the teacher. Explaining a concept to someone else is usually more helpful to the explainer than to the listener. So why not let the students do more teaching? That's one of the chief benefits of letting kids do the talking. This process is called interactive learning.

What is interactive learning? Interactive learning occurs when students discuss and work cooperatively in pairs or small groups.

Interactive learning encourages learners to work together. It honors the fact that students can learn from one another, not just from the teacher. Students work together in pairs or small groups to accomplish shared goals. They build together, discuss together, and present together. They teach each other and learn from one another. Success as a group is celebrated. Positive interdependence promotes individual and group learning.

Interactive learning not only helps people learn but also helps learners feel better about themselves and get along better with others. It accomplishes these things more effectively than the independent or competitive methods.

Here's a selection of interactive learning techniques that are used in Group's Core Belief Bible Study Series. With any of these models, leaders may assign students to specific partners or small groups. This will maximize cooperation and learning by preventing all the "rowdies" from linking up. And it will allow for new friendships to form outside of established cliques.

Following any period of partner or small-group work, the leader may reconvene the entire class for large-group processing. During this time the teacher may ask for reports or discoveries from individuals or teams. This technique builds in accountability for the teacherless pairs and small groups.

Pair-Share—With this technique each student turns to a partner and responds to a question or problem from the teacher or leader. Every learner responds. There are no passive observers. The teacher may then ask people to share their partners' responses.

Study Partners—Most curricula and most teachers call for Scripture passages to be read to the whole class by one person. One reads; the others doze.

Why not relinquish some teacher control and let partners read and react with each other? They'll all be involved—and will learn more.

Learning Groups—Students work together in small groups to create a model, design artwork, or study a passage or story; then they discuss what they learned through the experience. Each person in the learning group may be assigned a specific role. Here are some examples:

Reader

Recorder (makes notes of key thoughts expressed during the reading or discussion)

Checker (makes sure everyone understands and agrees with answers arrived at by the group)

Encourager (urges silent members to share their thoughts)

When everyone has a specific responsibility, knows what it is, and contributes to a small group, much is accomplished and much is learned.

Summary Partners—One student reads a paragraph, then the partner summarizes the paragraph or interprets its meaning. Partners alternate roles with each paragraph.

The paraphrasing technique also works well in discussions. Anyone who wishes to share a thought must first paraphrase what the previous person said. This sharpens listening skills and demonstrates the power of feedback communication.

Jigsaw—Each person in a small group examines a different concept, Scripture, or part of an issue. Then each teaches the others in the group. Thus, all members teach, and all must learn the others' discoveries. This technique is called a jigsaw because individuals are responsible to their group for different pieces of the puzzle.

JIGSAW EXAMPLE

Here's an example of a jigsaw.

Assign four-person teams. Have teammates each number off from one to four. Have all the Ones go to one corner of the room, all the Twos to another corner, and so on.

Tell team members they're responsible for learning information in their numbered corners and then for teaching their team members when they return to their original teams.

Give the following assignments to various groups:

Ones: Read Psalm 22. Discuss and list the prophecies made about Jesus.

Twos: Read Isaiah 52:13–53:12. Discuss and list the prophecies made about Jesus.

Threes: Read Matthew 27:1-32. Discuss and list the things that happened to Jesus.

Fours: Read Matthew 27:33-66. Discuss and list the things that happened to Jesus.

After the corner groups meet and discuss, instruct all learners to return to their original teams and report what they've learned. Then have each team determine which prophecies about Jesus were fulfilled in the passages from Matthew.

Call on various individuals in each team to report one or two prophecies that were fulfilled.

You Can Do It Too!

All this information may sound revolutionary to you, but it's really not. God has been using active and interactive learning to teach his people for generations. Just look at Abraham and Isaac, Jacob and Esau, Moses and the Israelites, Ruth and Boaz. And then there's Jesus, who used active learning all the time!

Group's Core Belief Bible Study Series makes it easy for you to use active and interactive learning with your group. The active and interactive elements are automatically built in! Just follow the outlines, and watch as your kids grow through experience and positive interaction with others.

> **FOR DEEPER STUDY**
>
> For more information on incorporating active and interactive learning into your work with teenagers, check out these resources:
>
> ● *Why Nobody Learns Much of Anything at Church: And How to Fix It,* by Thom and Joani Schultz (Group Publishing) and
> ● *Do It! Active Learning in Youth Ministry,* by Thom and Joani Schultz (Group Publishing).

your evaluation of

Bible Study Series
for senior high

why RELATIONSHIPS matter

Group Publishing, Inc.
Attention: Core Belief Talk-Back
P.O. Box 481
Loveland, CO 80539
Fax: (970) 679-4370

Please help us continue to provide innovative and useful resources for ministry. After you've led the studies in this volume, take a moment to fill out this evaluation; then mail or fax it to us at the address above. Thanks!

● ● ● ● ● ●

1. As a whole, this book has been (circle one)

not very helpful   very helpful
1   2   3   4   5   6   7   8   9   10

2. The best things about this book:

3. How this book could be improved:

4. What I will change because of this book:

5. Would you be interested in field-testing future Core Belief Bible Studies and giving us your feedback? If so, please complete the information below:

Name _____

Street address _____

City _____ State _____Zip _____

Daytime telephone (____) _____ Date _____

THANKS!

Permission to photocopy this evaluation from Group's Core Belief Bible Study Series granted for local church use.
Copyright © Group Publishing, Inc., P.O. Box 481, Loveland, CO 80539.

Bible Study Series

Give Your Teenagers a Solid Faith Foundation That Lasts a Lifetime!

Here are the *essentials* of the Christian life—core values teenagers *must* believe to make good decisions now...and build an *unshakable* lifelong faith. Developed by youth workers like you...field-tested with *real* youth groups in *real* churches...here's the meat your kids *must* have to grow spiritually—presented in a fun, involving way!

Each 4-session **Core Belief Bible Study Series** book lets you easily...
- Lead deep, compelling, *relevant* discussions your kids won't want to miss...
- Involve teenagers in exploring life-changing truths...
- Help kids create healthy relationships with each other—and you!

Plus you'll make an *eternal difference* in the lives of your kids as you give them a solid faith foundation that stands firm on God's Word.

Here are the Core Belief Bible Study Series titles already available...

Senior High Studies

Title	ISBN
Why **Authority** Matters	0-7644-0892-5
Why **Being a Christian** Matters	0-7644-0883-6
Why **Creation** Matters	0-7644-0880-1
Why **Forgiveness** Matters	0-7644-0887-9
Why **God** Matters	0-7644-0874-7
Why **God's Justice** Matters	0-7644-0886-0
Why **Jesus Christ** Matters	0-7644-0875-5
Why **Love** Matters	0-7644-0889-5
Why **Our Families** Matter	0-7644-0894-1
Why **Personal Character** Matters	0-7644-0885-2
Why **Prayer** Matters	0-7644-0893-3
Why **Relationships** Matter	0-7644-0896-8
Why **Serving Others** Matters	0-7644-0895-X
Why **Spiritual Growth** Matters	0-7644-0884-4
Why **Suffering** Matters	0-7644-0879-8
Why **the Bible** Matters	0-7644-0882-8
Why **the Church** Matters	0-7644-0890-9
Why **the Holy Spirit** Matters	0-7644-0876-3
Why **the Last Days** Matter	0-7644-0888-7
Why **the Spiritual Realm** Matters	0-7644-0881-X
Why **Worship** Matters	0-7644-0891-7

Junior High/Middle School Studies

Title	ISBN
The Truth About **Authority**	0-7644-0868-2
The Truth About **Being a Christian**	0-7644-0859-3
The Truth About **Creation**	0-7644-0856-9
The Truth About **Developing Character**	0-7644-0861-5
The Truth About **God**	0-7644-0850-X
The Truth About **God's Justice**	0-7644-0862-3
The Truth About **Jesus Christ**	0-7644-0851-8
The Truth About **Love**	0-7644-0865-8
The Truth About **Our Families**	0-7644-0870-4
The Truth About **Prayer**	0-7644-0869-0
The Truth About **Relationships**	0-7644-0872-0
The Truth About **Serving Others**	0-7644-0871-2
The Truth About **Sin and Forgiveness**	0-7644-0863-1
The Truth About **Spiritual Growth**	0-7644-0860-7
The Truth About **Suffering**	0-7644-0855-0
The Truth About **the Bible**	0-7644-0858-5
The Truth About **the Church**	0-7644-0899-2
The Truth About **the Holy Spirit**	0-7644-0852-6
The Truth About **the Last Days**	0-7644-0864-X
The Truth About **the Spiritual Realm**	0-7644-0857-7
The Truth About **Worship**	0-7644-0867-4

Order today from your local Christian bookstore, or write:
Group Publishing, P.O. Box 485, Loveland, CO 80539.

Exciting Resources for Your Youth Ministry

All-Star Games From All-Star Youth Leaders

The ultimate game book—from the biggest names in youth ministry! All-time no-fail favorites from Wayne Rice, Les Christie, Rich Mullins, Tiger McLuen, Darrell Pearson, Dave Stone, Bart Campolo, Steve Fitzhugh, and 21 others! You get all the games you'll need for any situation. Plus, you get practical advice about how to design your own games and tricks for turning a *good* game into a *great* game!

ISBN 0-7644-2020-8

Last Impressions: Unforgettable Closings for Youth Meetings

Make the closing moments of your youth programs powerful and memorable with this collection of Group's best-ever low-prep (or no-prep!) youth meeting closings. You get over 170 favorite closings, each tied to a thought-provoking Bible passage. Great for anyone who works with teenagers!

ISBN 1-55945-629-9

The Youth Worker's Encyclopedia of Bible-Teaching Ideas

Here are the most comprehensive idea-books available for youth workers. With more than 365 creative ideas in each of these 400-page encyclopedias, there's at least one idea for every book of the Bible. You'll find ideas for retreats and overnighters…learning games…adventures…special projects…affirmations…parties…prayers…music…devotions…skits…and more!

Old Testament	ISBN 1-55945-184-X
New Testament	ISBN 1-55945-183-1

PointMaker™ Devotions for Youth Ministry

These 45 PointMakers™ help your teenagers discover, understand, and apply biblical principles. Use PointMakers as brief meetings on specific topics or slide them into any youth curriculum to make a lasting impression. Includes handy Scripture and topical indexes that make it quick and easy to select the perfect PointMaker for any lesson you want to teach!

ISBN 0-7644-2003-8

Order today from your local Christian bookstore, or write: Group Publishing, P.O. Box 485, Loveland, CO 80539